From.

UNITED
WE
STAND

*Compiled by Elizabeth Poyet
and Virginia Reynolds*

 PETER PAUPER PRESS, INC.
White Plains, New York

*Ten percent of the publisher's proceeds from
the sale of this book will be donated to the*
**American Red Cross Liberty
Disaster Relief Fund.**
*Throughout its history, the
American Red Cross has helped the
American people in time of need.*

Designed by Heather Zschock

Text copyright © 2001
Peter Pauper Press, Inc.
202 Mamaroneck Avenue
White Plains, NY 10601
All rights reserved
ISBN 0-88088-745-1
Printed in China
7 6 5 4 3 2 1

Visit us at www.peterpauper.com

UNITED
WE
STAND

INTRODUCTION

FROM ITS VERY BEGINNINGS, our nation has embraced certain qualities: freedom, equality, moral courage, charity, and compassion for all. Since the earliest times, leaders and poets have sought to put these values into words. Their lines express what we, the people of America, think and feel about our beloved land. *United We Stand* includes the words of many distinguished leaders, orators, and literary figures: the women and men who have contributed so much to the greatness of this proud nation.

—E.P. and V.R.

Then join hand in hand, brave Americans all!
By uniting we stand, by dividing we fall.

JOHN DICKINSON

Where liberty dwells, there is my country.

BENJAMIN FRANKLIN

We never know how high we are
Till we are called to rise;
And then, if we are true to plan,
Our statures touch the skies.

EMILY DICKINSON

We confide in our strength, without boasting of it; we respect that of others, without fearing it.

THOMAS JEFFERSON

*You gain strength,
courage, and confidence
by every experience
in which you really stop
to look fear in the face.
…You must do the
thing which you think
you cannot do.*

ELEANOR ROOSEVELT

What the people want is very simple. They want an AMERICA as good as its promise.

BARBARA JORDAN

O LAND BEYOND COMPARE

I love thine inland seas,
Thy groves of giant trees,
    Thy rolling plains;
Thy rivers' mighty sweep,
Thy mystic canyons deep,
Thy mountains wild and steep,

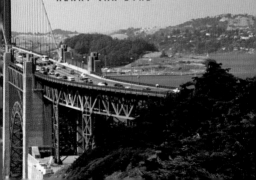

All thy domains;
Thy silver Eastern strands,
Thy Golden Gate that stands
Wide to the West;
Thy flowery Southland fair,
Thy sweet and crystal air,—
O land beyond compare,
Thee I love best!

HENRY VAN DYKE

Those who expect to reap the blessings of freedom must undergo the fatigue of supporting it.

THOMAS PAINE

None who have always been free can understand the terrible fascinating power of the hope of freedom to those who are not free.

PEARL S. BUCK

We in this country, in this generation, are, by destiny rather than choice, the watchmen on the walls of world freedom. We ask, therefore, that we may be worthy of our power and responsibility, that we may exercise

*our strength with wisdom
and restraint, and that
we may achieve in our
time and for all time the
ancient vision of*
**"peace on earth,
good will toward men."**

JOHN FITZGERALD KENNEDY

How difficult the task to quench the fire and the pride of private ambition, and to sacrifice ourselves and all our hopes and expectations to the public weal! How few have souls capable of so noble an undertaking! . . .

But there is a future recompense of reward, to which the upright man looks, and which he will most assuredly obtain, provided he perseveres unto the end.

ABIGAIL ADAMS

Liberty, when it begins to take root, is a plant of rapid growth.

GEORGE WASHINGTON

from **THE DECLARATION OF INDEPENDENCE**

We hold these truths to be self-evident; that all men are created equal; that they are endowed by their creator with certain unalienable rights; that among these are life, liberty, and the pursuit of happiness; that to secure these rights, governments are instituted among men, deriving their just powers from the

consent of the governed; that whenever any form of government becomes destructive to these ends, it is the right of the people to alter or to abolish it, and to institute new government, laying its foundation on such principles, and organizing its powers in such form, as to them shall seem most likely to effect their safety and happiness.

THOMAS JEFFERSON

FRIENDS, our people and our landmarks have been attacked, but the essence of America is indestructible. Our core principles— justice, liberty and democracy— will remain forever unscathed.

CONGRESSWOMAN NITA M. LOWEY

*In a chariot of light from
the region of the day,
The Goddess of Liberty came.
She brought in her hand
as a pledge of her love,
The plant she named*

Liberty Tree.

THOMAS PAINE

One man with courage makes a majority.

ANDREW JACKSON

Common sense is seeing things as they are; and doing things as they ought to be.

HARRIET BEECHER STOWE

Let us have faith that
right makes might,
and in that faith let us to
the end dare to do our
duty as we understand it.

ABRAHAM LINCOLN

The things that the flag stands for were created by the experiences of a great people. Everything that it stands for was written by their lives. The flag is the embodiment, not of sentiment, but of history. It represents the experiences made by men and women, the experiences of those who do and live under that flag.

WOODROW WILSON

It's better to light a candle than to curse the darkness.

ELEANOR ROOSEVELT

As long as our Government is administered **for the good of the people,** *and is regulated by their will . . . it will be worth defending.*

ANDREW JACKSON

I have passed the Rubicon, swim or sink, live or die, survive or perish with my country—that is my unalterable determination.

JOHN ADAMS

My fellow citizens of the world:

Ask not what America will do for you, but what together we can do for the freedom of man.

JOHN FITZGERALD KENNEDY

Equal rights for all, special privileges for none.

THOMAS JEFFERSON

WITH MALICE TOWARD NONE; with charity for all; with firmness in the right, as God gives us to see the right, let us strive on to finish the work we are in; to bind up the nation's wounds; to care for him who shall have borne the battle, and for his widow, and his orphan—to do all which may achieve and cherish a just and lasting peace among ourselves, and with all nations.

ABRAHAM LINCOLN

In the future days, which we seek to make secure, we look forward to a world founded upon four essential human freedoms:

The first is *freedom of speech and expression, everywhere in the world.*

The second is *freedom of every person to worship God in his own way, everywhere in the world.*

The third is
freedom from want,
everywhere in the world.
The fourth is
freedom from fear,
anywhere in the world.

FRANKLIN DELANO ROOSEVELT

*Now, gentlemen,
we must hang together,
or, assuredly,
we will all
hang separately.*

BENJAMIN FRANKLIN

I do not own an inch of land, But all I see is mine.

LUCY LARCOM

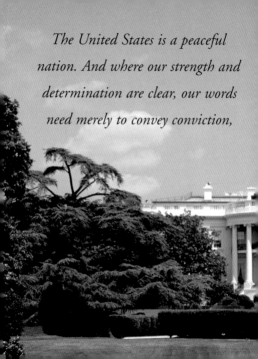

The United States is a peaceful nation. And where our strength and determination are clear, our words need merely to convey conviction,

not belligerence. If we are strong, our strength will speak for itself. If we are weak, words will be of no help.

JOHN FITZGERALD KENNEDY

I have a dream

that one day this nation
will rise up and live out the
true meaning of its creed:
*"We hold these truths
to be self-evident:
that all men
are created equal."* . . .

This will be the day when all of God's children will be able to sing with new meaning,

"My country, 'tis of thee,
Sweet land of liberty,
Of thee I sing;
Land where my fathers died,
Land of the pilgrims' pride,
From every mountainside,
Let freedom ring!"

DR. MARTIN LUTHER KING, JR.

Give me your tired, your poor,
Your huddled masses
yearning to breathe free,
The wretched refuse of
your teeming shore.
Send these, the homeless,
tempest-tost, to me;
I lift my lamp beside
the golden door!

EMMA LAZARUS

As the happiness of the
people is the sole end
of the government,
so the consent of the people
is the only foundation of it,
in reason, mortality,
and the natural
fitness of things.

JOHN ADAMS

. . . [R]eligion, or the duty which we owe to our Creator, and the manner of discharging it, can be directed only by reason and conviction, not by force or violence;

and therefore all men are equally entitled to the free exercise of religion, according to the dictates of conscience. . . [I]t is the mutual duty of all to practice . . . forbearance, love, and charity towards each other.

PATRICK HENRY

The experience of democracy is like the experience of life itself—always changing, infinite in its variety, sometimes turbulent and all the more valuable for having been tested by adversity.

JIMMY CARTER

*[Our] commitment to democracy
and self-government . . .
has set us apart from every society
that has ever existed because
of the longevity of our democracy
and the will of our people to
constantly renew ourselves.*

**U. S. SENATOR
HILLARY RODHAM CLINTON**

The ultimate determinant
in the struggle now going on
for the world will not be
bombs and rockets but
a test of wills and ideas—
a trial of spiritual resolve:
the values we hold,
the beliefs we cherish
and the ideals to which
we are dedicated.

RONALD REAGAN

What we demand . . . is nothing
peculiar to ourselves.
It is that the world
be made fit and
safe to live in;
and particularly that it be
made safe for every
peace-loving nation which,
like our own, wishes to live

its own life, determine its own institutions, be assured of JUSTICE AND FAIR DEALINGS BY THE OTHER PEOPLES OF THE WORLD, as against force and selfish aggression.

WOODROW WILSON

*The only thing
we have to fear
is fear itself.*

FRANKLIN DELANO ROOSEVELT

We Americans are a resilient, a determined and a patriotic nation. We will not lose the spirit that makes us the greatest democracy on earth . . .

U. S. SENATOR DIANNE FEINSTEIN

Together, let us build
sturdy mansions
of freedom,
mansions that all the
world can admire and copy,
but that no tyrant
can ever enter.

JOHN FITZGERALD KENNEDY

From

The Gettysburg Address

Four score and seven years ago our fathers brought forth on this continent a new nation, conceived in Liberty and dedicated to the proposition that all men are created equal ...

[W]e here highly resolve that these dead shall not have died in vain, that this nation, under God, shall have a new birth of freedom, and that government of the people, by the people, for the people, shall not perish from the earth.

ABRAHAM LINCOLN

We do not retreat.
We are not content to stand still.
As Americans, we go forward,
in the service of our country,
by the will of God.

FRANKLIN DELANO ROOSEVELT

Sometimes people call
me an idealist.
Well, that is the way I
know I am an American.
America is the
only idealistic nation
in the world.

WOODROW WILSON

The **United States** is not a nation of people which in the long run allows itself to be pushed around.

DOROTHY THOMPSON

*Men may die,
but the fabrics
of our free
institutions
remain unshaken.*

CHESTER ARTHUR

*We, too, born to freedom,
and believing in freedom,
are willing to fight to
maintain freedom.
We, and all others who
believe as deeply as we do,
would rather die on our feet
than live on our knees.*

FRANKLIN DELANO ROOSEVELT

Our flag has never waved over any community but in blessing.

WILLIAM MCKINLEY

The American spirit *is stronger than stone and mortar, tougher than steel and glass, and more enduring than any pain or suffering that can be inflicted on our national conscience.*

U. S. SENATOR OLYMPIA SNOWE

We are Americans.
That is a proud boast.
That is a great privilege,
to be a citizen of the
United States, and we must
meet our responsibilities.

We stand for freedom.
That is our conviction
for ourselves—that is our only
commitment to others.
No friend, no neutral and no
adversary should think otherwise.
We are not against any man—
or any nation—or any system—
except as it is hostile to freedom.

JOHN FITZGERALD KENNEDY

Our reliance is in the love
of liberty which God
has planted in us.
Our defense is in the spirit
which prized liberty as
the heritage of all men,
in all lands, everywhere.

ABRAHAM LINCOLN

I believe that America today stands between hope and history— at the edge of a moment when these two powerful forces are as one, when we can embrace

the dawn of the new century,
drawing strength and
guidance from our past,
filled with confidence that
in this new age of possibility,
our best is yet to come.

WILLIAM JEFFERSON CLINTON

America is a nation full of good fortune, with so much to be grateful for.

But we are not spared from suffering. In every generation, the world has produced enemies of human freedom.

They have attacked America,
because we are freedom's
home and defender.
And the commitment
of our fathers is now the
calling of our time.

PRESIDENT GEORGE W. BUSH

America the Beautiful

O beautiful for spacious skies,
For amber waves of grain,
For purple mountain majesties
Above the fruited plain!
America! America!
God shed His grace on thee.
And crown thy good with brotherhood
From sea to shining to sea!

KATHARINE LEE BATES

PHOTO CREDITS